TIMOR-LESTE 2016 HUMAN RIGHTS REPORT

EXECUTIVE SUMMARY

Timor-Leste is a multiparty, parliamentary republic. Following free, fair, and relatively peaceful elections in 2012, Taur Matan Ruak was elected president and head of state and Kay Rala Xanana Gusmao became prime minister of a three-party coalition government. In February 2015, Gusmao resigned and, in a peaceful transition, Dr. Rui Maria de Araujo of the opposition FRETILIN party (Revolutionary Front for an Independent East Timor) became prime minister.

Civilian control of security forces remained weak.

Significant human rights problems included security force abuses, gender-based and domestic violence, and land tenure and expropriation concerns.

Other human rights problems included a lack of due process due to a weak judicial system, impingements on freedom of assembly, trafficking in persons, and ineffective workers' rights protections.

The government took some steps to prosecute members and officials of the security services who used excessive force, but public perceptions of impunity persisted.

Section 1. Respect for the Integrity of the Person, Including Freedom from:

a. Arbitrary Deprivation of Life and other Unlawful or Politically Motivated Killings

There was at least one report that the government or its agents committed arbitrary or unlawful killings. Border Police Unit officers stationed in Cova Lima district allegedly shot and killed a man with a mental disability in August. Police were conducting an internal investigation into the killing, which had not concluded by September. Human rights organizations were not aware of any cases based on allegations of unlawful killings in the previous year, and the Prosecutor General's Office stated there was insufficient evidence for trial but it was unable to comment on whether the investigations continued or the case had been closed.

b. Disappearance

There were no reports of politically motivated disappearances.

c. Torture and Other Cruel, Inhuman, or Degrading Treatment or Punishment

The law prohibits such practices and limits the situations in which police officers may resort to physical force and the use of firearms. During the year there were multiple reports of the use of excessive force by security forces. Most complaints involved maltreatment, use of excessive force during incident response or arrest, and threats made at gunpoint.

For example, in January police officers from the Public Order Battalion stationed in Maliana reportedly beat a medical staff member on duty in the hospital who attempted to interfere with their harsh treatment of a patient. Police leaders responded by opening an investigation into the incident, and the case was in process in Suai District Court.

Prison and Detention Center Conditions

Prison and detention center conditions generally did not meet international standards, and the larger of the country's two prisons was overcrowded.

Physical Conditions: According to human rights monitoring organizations, police station detention cells generally did not comply with international standards and lacked sanitation facilities and bedding, although the police were making efforts to improve them. The prison in Dili (Becora) was overcrowded. It had an estimated capacity of 290 inmates, but in September held 555 adult and juvenile male convicts and pretrial detainees. According to independent monitoring, juvenile and adult prisoners were in the same block, although separate blocks housed pretrial detainees and convicts. Gleno Prison was not overcrowded, but held women as well as adult male convicts and pretrial detainees, albeit in separate blocks. Conditions were the same for male and female prisoners, who shared recreation areas. Housing blocks separated nonviolent offenders from violent offenders. There were no specific supports for offenders with mental disabilities.

Authorities provided food three times daily in the prisons; however, there was no budget for food in police station detention centers, and officers and independent monitors reported that police purchased food for prisoners out of their personal funds. While authorities provided water in prisons, it was not always available in detention centers. Due to lack of Ministry of Health staff, the Ombudsman for

Human Rights and Justice (PDHJ) found that there was no regular staffing of medical centers at the hospitals and medical staff might only be available on a weekly or monthly basis at the facility. For urgent cases and those beyond basic needs, authorities took inmates to a local hospital in Gleno or Dili. Access to clean restroom facilities was generally sufficient, although without significant privacy. PDHJ assessed ventilation and lighting as adequate in prisons, but not in detention centers. Prisoners were able to exercise for two hours daily.

Administration: Independent monitors reported that prison authorities followed case management guidelines and standard operating procedures to track prisoners. Prisoners and detainees could submit complaints to judicial authorities without censorship and request investigation of credible allegations of problematic conditions. The PDHJ oversees prison conditions and prisoner welfare. It monitored inmates in Dili, and reported that the government was generally responsive to recommendations. Nonetheless, some human rights monitoring organizations questioned how widely known the complaint mechanism was and whether prisoners felt free to utilize it. Prisoners were able to practice their religion without significant restrictions.

Prisons permit 30-minute visits twice per week, but some visitors complained that the duration was too short, given the time required to travel for the visit.

Independent Monitoring: The government permitted prison visits by nongovernmental organizations (NGOs) and independent human rights observers.

Improvements: Authorities completed construction of a new prison on the south coast, to be occupied early in 2017.

d. Arbitrary Arrest or Detention

The law prohibits arbitrary arrest and detention, and the government generally observed these prohibitions.

Role of the Police and Security Apparatus

The law does not fully clarify the roles of the national police (PNTL), the judicially mandated Scientific Police for Criminal Investigations, and the military (F-FDTL). Security sector experts also said that the operational roles and relationship between the PNTL and the F-FDTL were unclear.

The PNTL is legally responsible for law enforcement and maintenance of order within the country. It has several specialized units, including border, maritime, and immigration units.

The F-FDTL is legally responsible for external security, and may play a role in internal security only in "crisis" or "emergency" situations declared by the government and president. The F-FDTL, however, may support police in joint operations if requested by a "competent entity." The president is commander-in-chief of the armed forces, but the chief of defense, the F-FDTL's senior military officer, exercised day-to-day command over the armed forces. F-FDTL military police responded occasionally to incidents involving only civilians.

During the year multiple clashes between members of the police and military took place. For example, in August an off-duty PNTL officer in Ainaro shot an off-duty F-FDTL officer with his service weapon. The PNTL subsequently fired the officer, and the Prosecutor's Office was conducting a criminal investigation. During the year security forces undertook only ad hoc investigations into specific incidents.

According to expert sources, civilian oversight of the PNTL and the F-FDTL remained relatively weak. Various bilateral partners continued efforts to strengthen the development of the police, especially through community policing programs and technical assistance efforts, including work to improve disciplinary and accountability mechanisms within the PNTL.

The PNTL's internal accountability mechanisms remained somewhat ineffective, but improved. Rates of reported cases closed without investigation decreased, but the office responsible for internal affairs (the PNTL Department of Justice) did not have sufficient resources to investigate and respond to all cases brought to its attention. The office increased its use of disciplinary measures, including demotions, written admonitions, and fines. Nonetheless, especially outside the capital, district commanders may not fully engage in the disciplinary process, perhaps due partly to lack of familiarity with disciplinary procedures.

The internal affairs office may recommend that the Commander General refer cases to the Office of the Prosecutor General for investigation. The office reported 35 investigations during the year, including some from the previous year, of which 21 were still under investigation, 13 had been closed, and one had been transferred to the Prosecutor General's Office for criminal investigation.

F-FDTL regulations permit referral of disciplinary incidents amounting to crimes to the prosecutor general (misconduct is processed internally). One security sector NGO assessed the F-FDTL's disciplinary system as strong but not entirely free of political influence.

Citizens reported obstacles to reporting complaints about police behavior, including repeated requests to return later or to submit their complaints in writing.

There was a widespread belief that members of the security forces enjoyed substantial immunity for illegal or abusive actions. During the year, nonetheless, a criminal trial of F-FDTL officers accused of beating a civilian to death in Laivai in 2010 took place in Baucau District Court; two officers were convicted and three found innocent. The officers also were discharged from the military.

Arrest Procedures and Treatment of Detainees

The law requires judicial warrants prior to arrests or searches, except in exceptional circumstances or in cases of flagrante delicto; one reported violation of this provision involved an unauthorized raid on a home (see section 1.f.).

The law requires a hearing within 72 hours of arrest to review the lawfulness of an arrest or detention. During these hearings the judge may also determine whether the suspect should be released because conditions for pretrial detention had not been met, released conditionally (usually after posting some form of collateralized bail or on condition that the suspect report regularly to police), or whether the case should be dismissed due to lack of evidence. While the government's 2014 decision to rescind visas for international legal advisors, who had filled critical roles as judges, prosecutors, and investigators, continued to affect the justice system, backlogs decreased during the year, particularly in courts outside of Dili. Justice sector monitoring organizations reported that the system adhered much more closely to the 72-hour timeline than in past years.

Time in pretrial detention may be deducted from a final sentence, but there is no remedy in cases that do not result in conviction.

The law provides for access to legal representation at all stages of the proceedings and provisions exist for providing public defenders for all defendants at no cost (see section 1.e.). Due to a lack of human resources and transportation, however, public defenders were not always able to attend to their clients and sometimes met clients for the first time during their first court hearing.

<u>Pretrial Detention</u>: The law specifies that a person may be held in pretrial detention for up to one year without presentation of an indictment, two years without a first-instance conviction, or three years without a final conviction on appeal. If any of these deadlines are not met, the detained person may file a claim for release. Exceptionally complex cases can also provide justification for the extension of each of those limits by up to six months with permission of a judge. Pretrial detainees composed approximately 20 percent of the total prison population. Procedural delays and staff shortages were the most frequent causes of trial delays. In many cases, the length of pretrial detention equaled or exceeded the length of the sentence upon conviction.

<u>Detainee's Ability to Challenge Lawfulness of Detention before a Court</u>: While persons arrested or detained may challenge the legal basis of their detention and obtain prompt release, justice sector monitoring organizations reported that such challenges rarely occur, likely due to limited knowledge of the provision allowing such challenges.

e. Denial of Fair Public Trial

The law provides that judges shall perform their duties "independently and impartially without improper influence" and requires public prosecutors to discharge their duties impartially. Many legal sector observers expressed concern about the independence of some judicial organs in politically sensitive cases, a severe shortage of qualified personnel, and the complex legal regime influenced by the Portuguese, Indonesian, UN administration, and various other international norms. An additional problem is that all laws and many trial proceedings and court documents are in Portuguese, a language spoken by approximately 10 percent of the population. Nonetheless, observers noted that citizens generally enjoyed a fair, although not always expeditious, trial and that the judiciary was largely independent.

Administrative failings involving the bench, prosecution, and/or defense led to prolonged delays in trials. Moreover, the law requires at least one international judge on a panel in some cases, which has, after the 2014 cancellation of foreign judges' contracts, created substantial delays.

Trial Procedures

Under the criminal procedure code, defendants enjoy a presumption of innocence, access to a lawyer, the right against self-incrimination, and to attend their trial. Trials are held before judges or judicial panels; juries are not used. Defendants can confront hostile witnesses and present other witnesses and evidence. Defendants and their attorneys have access to government-held evidence and have a right of appeal to higher courts. The government provides interpretation, as necessary, into local languages. Observers noted that the courts made significant progress in providing interpretation services during court proceedings. The highest court in the country has held that immediate family members cannot refuse to testify against another family member, where the crime is a public crime and the immediate family member is the victim, a decision criticized by civil society organizations.

Justice sector NGOs expressed concern that judges did not provide clear information or take the time to explain and read their decisions. Observers also noted that in many cases judges did not follow the Law on Witnesses, which provides important protections for witnesses. Additionally, the country has not passed juvenile justice legislation, leaving many juveniles in the justice system without protections and perhaps subject to vigilante justice by frustrated communities seeking justice.

The constitution contemplates a supreme court, but it has not yet been established due to staffing and resource limits. The Court of Appeals carries out supreme court functions.

A mobile court based in Dili operated in areas that did not have a permanent court. The court processed only pretrial proceedings.

For crimes considered "semi-public," some citizens utilized traditional (customary) systems of justice that did not necessarily follow due process standards or provide witness protection, but provided convenient and speedy reconciliation proceedings with which the population felt comfortable.

The public defender's office, concentrated in Dili, was too small to meet the need, and many defendants relied on lawyers provided by legal aid organizations. A number of defendants who were assigned public defenders reported they never saw their lawyers, and some observers noted that few defenders viewed their role as client advocates or were confused about their duties to the client versus the state. Public defenders did not have access to transportation to visit clients in detention, so sometimes met their clients for the first time in court.

Political Prisoners and Detainees

There were no reports of political prisoners or detainees.

Civil Judicial Procedures and Remedies

As there is no separate civil judicial system in the country, civil litigation experienced the same problems encountered in the criminal justice system. No regional human rights body has jurisdiction in Timor-Leste.

Property Restitution

There is no comprehensive national legislation on land rights and the government was criticized for disregarding many private claims and evicting some residents from land defined as public property or for which title was unclear. During the year the government expropriated an undisclosed number of homes in connection with large development projects in Oecusse and Suai. In Oecusse, NGOs and media reported evictions with varying compensation, sometimes including building materials and labor costs for new homes in alternate locations. In Suai, communities complained that they were given some compensation but that they were led to believe additional funds and government support would be forthcoming. The Suai communities also complained that the alternative housing provided by the government did not meet community standards and that the relocations significantly changed their livelihoods and cultural systems.

The lack of a legal framework also led to land acquisition by means, such as payment to undocumented occupants of the land or purported owners, which may not hold up once parliament adopts a land law.

f. Arbitrary or Unlawful Interference with Privacy, Family, Home, or Correspondence

The law prohibits arbitrary interference with privacy, family, home, or correspondence. In one reported case, in August police and F-FDTL personnel entered the home of a prominent resistance veteran without appropriate authorization and harassed his family. Security force officials claimed they had no advance knowledge of the raid and were investigating the allegations. Observers also noted a general lack of privacy protections throughout the government, particularly in the health sector.

Section 2. Respect for Civil Liberties, Including:

a. Freedom of Speech and Press

The constitution provides for freedom of speech and press, and the government generally respected these rights. Independent media were active and expressed a wide variety of views without restriction.

Press and Media Freedoms: While journalists continued to voice concerns about the 2014 media law, which they view as unnecessarily restrictive, there were no reports of the law being used to restrict press freedoms during the reporting period. The Press Council, responsible for monitoring media under the law, took office in May. Two council members were selected by journalists, one by media owners, and two by Parliament.

In July a PNTL traffic officer reportedly hit a *Business Post* journalist for taking pictures in the Colmera neighborhood in Dili. The incident drew swift condemnation from the journalists' association, the prime minister, and the president. The PNTL took initial disciplinary measures against the officer, with additional action awaiting the results of a criminal investigation.

Libel/Slander Laws: The prime minister, as a private citizen, requested the Prosecutor's Office investigate *Timor Post* and journalist Raimundos Oki for "calumnious defamation" following a 2015 article alleging that the prime minister, while an advisor to the Ministry of Finance, used improper influence in a contracting decision. The newspaper later admitted the article contained factual errors. The trial began December 5.

Internet Freedom

The government did not restrict or disrupt access to the internet or censor online content, and there were no credible reports that the government monitored private online communications without appropriate legal authority. Politicians at various times suggested the government was considering restricting access to certain websites, but no such action was taken. While improving, internet access remained prohibitively expensive or unavailable for most, especially outside urban areas. Reliable data on accessibility remained unavailable.

Academic Freedom and Cultural Events

There were no government restrictions on academic freedom or cultural events. The National Language Institute must approve academic research on Tetum and other indigenous languages and regularly did so.

b. Freedom of Peaceful Assembly and Association

Freedom of Assembly

The constitution guarantees "freedom to assemble peacefully and without weapons, without a need for prior authorization." The law on assembly and demonstrations establishes guidelines on obtaining permits to hold demonstrations, requires police be notified five days in advance of any demonstration or strike, and establishes setback requirements at some buildings. The power to grant or deny permits is vested only in the PNTL. According to the PDHJ, in Ermera, PNTL officers and FRETILIN party members broke up a veterans' organization assembly. In January during the state visit of Indonesian President Joko Widodo, the government banned protests.

Freedom of Association

The constitution guarantees freedom of association, although the government continued to pursue cases against members of two armed opposition organizations (the KRM and the CPD-RDTL) declared illegal in a March 2014 parliamentary resolution.

c. Freedom of Religion

See the Department of State's *International Religious Freedom Report* at www.state.gov/religiousfreedomreport/.

d. Freedom of Movement, Internally Displaced Persons, Protection of Refugees, and Stateless Persons

The law provides for freedom of internal movement, foreign travel, emigration, and repatriation, and the government generally respected these rights.

In-country Movement: The government occasionally established checkpoints for various law enforcement purposes at locations around the country.

Protection of Refugees

<u>Access to Asylum</u>: The law provides for granting asylum or refugee status; however, the system is not in line with international standards. There were concerns regulations governing asylum and refugee status may preclude genuine refugees from proving their eligibility for such status. For example, persons who wish to apply for asylum have only 72 hours to do so after entering the country. Foreign nationals already present in the country have only 72 hours to initiate the process after the situation in their home country becomes too dangerous for a safe return.

Section 3. Freedom to Participate in the Political Process

The constitution and law provide citizens the ability to choose their government in free and fair periodic elections held by secret ballot and based on universal and equal suffrage for those 17 and older.

Elections and Political Participation

<u>Recent Elections</u>: The most recent presidential and parliamentary elections took place in 2012, with UN assistance. International observers assessed them as free and fair. Voter turnout was 74 percent, down from 80 percent in 2007. Some individuals complained they were disenfranchised by a rule requiring voters to vote only in the village in which they registered. There were no procedures for international or absentee voting. Serious concerns about possible pre- and post-election violence proved largely unfounded and, unlike in 2007, the formation of the new government occurred in relatively peaceful circumstances. In February 2015, Prime Minister Xanana Gusmao resigned, and Dr. Rui Maria de Araujo of the opposition FRETILIN party became prime minister in a peaceful transition of power.

Following revisions to the local elections and the electoral management bodies laws, local elections were held in October and November. While there were several complaints about voting logistics, including incomplete voter registration lists and improper ballot provision, the elections were generally seen as free and fair.

<u>Political Parties and Political Participation</u>: Establishment of new political parties is difficult, as regulations require new parties to obtain 20,000 signatures, which must also include at least 1,000 signatures from each of the 13 districts, to register.

<u>Participation of Women and Minorities</u>: Electoral laws require at least one-third of candidates on party lists be women. Women held more than a third of seats in Parliament and several ministerial, vice-ministerial, and secretary of state positions. At the local level, at least three women must serve on every village council, which generally include 10 to 20 representatives, depending on village size. In the local elections, the number of female village chiefs increased from 11 to 21. Meaningful participation by women at the national and local levels, even when elected, is sometimes constrained by traditional attitudes and stereotypes.

The country's few ethnic minority groups were well integrated into the political system. The number of members of these groups in parliament and other government positions was uncertain, since self-identification of ethnicity was not a common practice.

Section 4. Corruption and Lack of Transparency in Government

The penal code provides criminal penalties for official corruption. The government faced many challenges in implementing the law, and the perception that officials frequently engaged in corrupt practices was widespread.

The government continued steps to fight corruption by undertaking surprise inspections of government-run programs, increasing pressure to implement asset management and transparency systems, and making this a top priority.

<u>Corruption</u>: The Anti-Corruption Commission (CAC) is legally charged with leading national anticorruption activities and has the authority to refer cases for prosecution. Although the CAC is independent, its budget is controlled by the government and can be changed, making the CAC vulnerable to political pressures.

During the year the CAC addressed several corruption cases. A high-profile case against former minister of finance Emilia Pires continued in Dili District Court, although Pires' absence from the country and apparent refusal to return led the court to postpone the trial's resumption multiple times.

There were accusations of police, including border police, involvement in corruption--most commonly bribery and abuse of power. Anecdotally, corruption was widespread among government officials. Allegations of nepotism in government hiring were common. The customs service was under scrutiny for alleged corruption related to incoming goods, but no cases have been filed. The

National Risk Assessment of Money Laundering and Terrorist Financing, published in October, called corruption endemic.

Financial Disclosure: The law requires that the highest members of government declare their assets to the Court of Appeals, but the declarations do not have to be made public and there are no criminal penalties for noncompliance. The president made his fourth public asset disclosure in September.

Public Access to Information: The law stipulates that all legislation, supreme court decisions (when the court is established), and decisions made by government bodies must be published in the official gazette. If not published, they are invalid. Regulations also provide for public access to court proceedings and decisions and the national budget and accounts. Many documents, however, are only published in Portuguese. Moreover, obtaining hard copies entails a small fee and (often burdensome) travel to the printing office. The government publishes documents online; however, the internet is expensive and not widely available.

By law all government contracts and financial information are published on the online Transparency Portal. Some have complained that the website does not provide a narrative report from which one may determine spending.

Parliament held fewer closed sessions during the year and requested commentary from the public and NGOs on several key pieces of legislation, including a pending land law package. Information on the government's Suai and Oecusse development projects was difficult to obtain.

Section 5. Governmental Attitude Regarding International and Nongovernmental Investigation of Alleged Violations of Human Rights

A wide variety of domestic and international human rights groups generally operated without government restriction, investigating and publishing their findings on human rights cases. Government officials usually cooperated with these organizations, although the government did not always respond to their recommendations.

The country's efforts to redress human rights abuses committed during the Indonesian occupation have been criticized as insufficient and ineffective. The government supported NGOs that organized an event in November to bring 13 children taken to Indonesia during the occupation back to meet their families in Timor-Leste.

During the January visit of Indonesian President Joko Widodo, the police intelligence service and other members of the security forces allegedly harassed Yayasan HAK, the country's leading human rights NGO, which had been planning to publish a press release asking Indonesia not to forget crimes committed during the Indonesian occupation. The government posted a strong security presence at the organization's offices throughout the visit. The organization submitted a complaint to the prosecutor's office.

Government Human Rights Bodies: By law the independent PDHJ is responsible for the promotion of human rights and good governance and has its own budget and dedicated staff. It has the power to investigate and monitor human rights abuses and governance standards as well as make recommendations, including for prosecution, to relevant authorities. The PDHJ has satellite offices in Manufahi, Maliana, Oecusse, and Baucau. During the year the office investigated and monitored land evictions, access to justice, governance, prisoner complaints, and abuse by security forces. There were no reports of significant government interference. The PDHJ, in cooperation with the UN, provided human rights training to the PNTL and signed an agreement to do the same for the F-FDTL.

Section 6. Discrimination, Societal Abuses, and Trafficking in Persons

Women

Rape and Domestic Violence: Gender-based violence remained a serious concern. In a study published in May, the Asia Foundation found that 59 percent of girls and women between 15 and 49 years old had experienced sexual or physical violence at the hands of an intimate partner and that 14 percent of girls and women had been raped by someone other than a partner. Although rape, including marital rape, is a crime punishable by up to 20 years in prison, failures to investigate or prosecute cases of alleged rape and sexual abuse were common. The formal justice system addressed an increasing number of reported domestic and sexual abuse cases, reflecting increased knowledge by community leaders and police officers that gender-based violence is a public crime that may not be dealt with through traditional justice mechanisms.

The Law Against Domestic Violence broadly covers all forms of domestic violence, including marital rape, and augments the Penal Code. While many cultural and institutional obstacles hinder implementation of the law, local NGOs viewed the law as having a positive effect by encouraging victims of domestic violence to report their cases to police. The secretary of state for the support and socioeconomic promotion of women has a gender focal point in each district, which helps direct victims to appropriate resources and supports capacity building and key actors in their areas.

According to the Office of the Prosecutor General, domestic violence offenses were the second-most commonly charged crimes in the criminal justice system, after simple assault. Several NGOs that monitored the courts' treatment of such cases, and those providing services to victims in such cases, criticized the failure to issue protection orders and over-reliance on suspended sentences, even in cases involving significant bodily harm. Prosecutors routinely charged cases involving aggravated injury and use of deadly weapons as low-level simple assaults.

Police, prosecutors, and judges routinely ignored many parts of the law that protect victims. NGOs noted that fines were paid to the court and often came from shared family resources, further hurting the victim. Between January and August, however, judges sentenced defendants convicted of domestic violence offenses to incarceration in at least nine cases, a significant increase over the previous year.

The PNTL's Vulnerable Persons Units (VPUs) generally handled cases of domestic violence and sexual crimes. The unit, however, does not have enough staff to provide a significant presence in all areas of the country, necessitating the involvement of other police units, especially community police, who are commonly present at the village level. Women's organizations considered VPU performance as variable but improved.

The government and civil society actively promoted awareness campaigns and provided training to government responders to combat all forms of violence against women.

The Ministry of Social Solidarity is charged with providing assistance to victims of domestic violence. During the year ministry staff in each district included a gender-based violence focal point to coordinate a referral network, a coordinator for the Bolsa de Mae (Mother's Purse) support fund, and two additional staff who focused on children's issues. Due to staff shortages, the ministry had difficulty responding to all cases. To deal with this problem, the ministry worked closely with local NGOs and service providers to offer assistance to victims of violence, including shelters, a safe room at the national hospital, financial and food support, and escorts to judicial proceedings.

<u>Sexual Harassment</u>: The labor code prohibits sexual harassment in the work place, but such harassment reportedly was widespread. Relevant authorities processed no such cases during the year (see section 7.d.).

<u>Reproductive Rights</u>: Couples and individuals have the right to decide the number, spacing, and timing of their children; manage their reproductive health; and have access to the means to do so free from discrimination, coercion, and violence. Economic, cultural, and religious considerations and distance (in rural areas) sometimes limited women's reproductive rights. Unmarried girls and women under age 20, for example, may be denied reproductive health services. Additionally, in many areas, service providers sometimes required a husband's permission before providing reproductive health services. Healthcare was not readily available for complications associated with abortion due to overall lack of women's healthcare and the criminalization of abortion.

According to estimates from the UN Population Division, 27.2 percent of women of reproductive age used a modern form of contraception. The Ministry of Health and NGOs promoted both natural and modern family planning methods, including the distribution of intrauterine devices, injectable contraceptives, and condoms, although government efforts heavily focused on natural methods. NGOs noted government clinics lacked the capacity and understanding to dispense some contraceptives properly and that clinics often lacked contraceptive stocks. Local service providers provided more than 50 percent of reproductive services.

According to 2015 World Health Organization estimates, the average maternal mortality rate in the country was 215 deaths per 100,000 live births. Access to maternal health services remained a challenge for persons in rural areas, although each district has at least one medical facility that provides maternal care. Sixty-one percent of mothers received antenatal care from a medical professional, and 32 percent of mothers received post-partum care. Recent efforts by the government and NGOs have expanded access to midwives and other skilled professionals, in addition to increasing access to information and use of breastfeeding.

<u>Discrimination</u>: The constitution states that "women and men shall have the same rights and duties in all areas of family life and political, economic, social, cultural life," but it does not specifically address discrimination.

Some customary practices discriminate against women, including traditional inheritance systems that tend to exclude women from land ownership. There have been complaints that the company registering land claims used forms that do not protect women's rights to property or follow best practice related to gender.

Other cultural practices, such as payment of a bride price as part of marriage agreements (barlake), also occurred in some areas and have been linked to domestic violence and to the inability to leave an abusive relationship. Additionally, in some communities a widow was forced to marry one of their husband's family members or leave their husband's home if they did not have children together.

Some women reported employment discrimination based on marital status (see section 7.d.).

The Secretary of State for the Support and Socio-Economic Promotion of Women is responsible for the promotion of gender equality. Several NGOs focused on women's issues and collaborated in a powerful network.

Children

Birth Registration: Children acquire citizenship through birth within the country or by having a citizen parent or grandparent. A central civil registry lists a child's name at birth and issues birth certificates. The rate of birth registration was low, especially in rural areas, but increasing. The government reported that children separated from their parents or those whose biological father is unknown have the right to access the registry through other responsible family members. There were no reports of discrimination based on birth registration. While access to services such as schooling does not depend on birth registration, birth registration is necessary to acquire a passport. Registration later in life requires only a reference from the village chief.

Education: The constitution stipulates that primary education shall be compulsory and free. The law requires nine years of compulsory education beginning at six years of age; however, there is no system to enforce attendance, nor is there a system to ensure that the provision of education is free. Language issues and teacher quality hampered the education system. Dropout rates were often very high due to distance, malnutrition, teenage pregnancy, or lack of parental support. While public schools were tuition-free, students paid for supplies and uniforms. The most recent UN and government statistics available (2010) indicated that approximately 20 to 30 percent of primary school-age children nationwide were not enrolled in school, with non-enrollment substantially higher in rural than in urban areas. While initial attendance rates for boys and girls were similar, girls often were forced to leave school if they became pregnant and faced difficulty in obtaining school documents or transferring schools. Lack of sanitation facilities at some schools also led some girls to drop out upon reaching puberty.

<u>Child Abuse</u>: The law protects against child abuse; however, abuse in many forms was common. Sexual abuse of children remained a serious concern. Despite widespread reports of child abuse, few cases entered the judicial system. Observers criticized the courts for handing down shorter sentences than prescribed by law in numerous cases of sexual abuse of children during the year. NGOs and some parliamentarians were vocal on the need for a comprehensive law on incest, but none has been passed.

While the Ministry of Education has a nominal zero tolerance policy for corporal punishment, there is no law on the issue, and reports indicated the practice was common. An organization working on children's rights found that in 87 schools across six districts, an average of three cases of corporal punishment were reported every day at each school.

<u>Early and Forced Marriage</u>: Although a marriage cannot be registered until the younger spouse is at least age 16, cultural, religious and civil marriages were recognized in the civil code. Cultural pressure to marry, especially if a girl or woman becomes pregnant, was strong. Underage couples cannot officially marry, but are often married de facto once they have children together. Forced marriage rarely occurred, although reports indicated that social pressure sometimes encouraged victims of rape to marry their attacker or persons to enter into an arranged marriage where a bride price was paid According to the most recent information from UNICEF (2010), an estimated 19 percent of girls married prior to the age of 18.

<u>Sexual Exploitation of Children</u>: Sexual assault against children was a significant problem, but one that cultural taboos left largely unaddressed. Some commercial sexual exploitation of children also occurred. The penal code makes sexual conduct by an adult with anyone below the age of 17 a crime, and increases penalties when such conduct involves victims younger than 14. The penal code also makes both child prostitution and child pornography crimes, but defines a "child" for purposes of those provisions as a "minor less than 17 years of age," leaving 17-year-old children vulnerable to commercial sexual exploitation. The penal code also criminalizes abduction of a minor.

There were reports that child victims of sexual abuse were sometimes forced to testify in public fora despite a witness protection law that provides for video link or other secure testimony.

International Child Abductions: The country is not a party to the 1980 Hague Convention on the Civil Aspects of International Child Abduction. See the Department of State's Annual Report on International Parental Abduction at travel.state.gov/content/childabduction/en/legal/compliance.html.

Anti-Semitism

There was no indigenous Jewish population, and there were no reports of anti-Semitic acts.

Trafficking in Persons

See the Department of State's Trafficking in Persons Report at www.state.gov/j/tip/rls/tiprpt/.

Persons with Disabilities

The constitution grants equal rights to and prohibits discrimination against persons with disabilities in addition to requiring the state to protect them. No specific legislation addresses the rights and/or support of persons with disabilities.

The Ministry of Social Solidarity is responsible for protecting the rights of persons with disabilities. The Ministry of Health is responsible for treating mental disabilities. In many districts, children with disabilities were unable to attend school due to accessibility problems. There were no special educational services for children with mental or learning disabilities. Training and vocational initiatives did not address the needs of persons with disabilities.

Electoral regulations provide accommodations, including personal assistance, to enable persons with disabilities to vote.

Service providers noted that domestic violence and sexual assault against persons with disabilities was a growing concern. They indicated further that such cases had been slow to receive support from the justice sector. Persons with mental disabilities accused of crimes are entitled to special protections by law. The public defender worked closely with the police to ensure suspects with mental disabilities received prompt access to a lawyer and prosecution worked to ensure proper protections in proceedings. Prisons do not have specific supports for persons with mental disabilities.

There were reports that persons with mental disabilities sometimes faced discriminatory or degrading treatment due in part to a lack of appropriate community support or lack of referral to existing resources. There was a deficit of qualified psychologists in the country, and no long-term treatment facilities for those with mental disabilities. There is one Ministry of Health professional per district; however, lack of transportation hinders access. District offices often did not have sufficient supplies of drugs, and many with mental disabilities had to wait several months for drugs.

National/Racial/Ethnic Minorities

Long-standing tensions between persons from the eastern districts (Lorosa'e) and western districts (Loromonu) seemed to have eased, and observers reported no incidents. Anger toward the Chinese minority continued, especially due to resentment over their perceived economic advantages. Communities and politicians called for stricter regulations on Chinese businesses and for better enforcement of laws against persons working in-country on tourist visas, a perceived pattern among Chinese visitors.

Acts of Violence, Discrimination, and Other Abuses Based on Sexual Orientation and Gender Identity

The constitution and law are silent on same-sex relations and other matters of sexual orientation and gender identity. The PDHJ worked with civil society organization CODIVA (Coalition on Diversity and Action) to increase awareness in the lesbian, gay, bisexual, transgender, and intersex (LGBTI) community regarding processes available for human rights complaints. While physical abuse in public or by public authorities was uncommon, LGBTI persons were often verbally abused and discriminated against in some public services, including medical centers. CODIVA noted that transgender members of the community were particularly vulnerable to harassment and discrimination. Those working with LGBTI individuals noted that abuse most commonly occurred within the family.

Access to education was limited for some LGBTI individuals who were removed from the family home or who feared abuse at school. Transgender students were

more likely to experience bullying and drop out of school at the secondary level.
Several openly gay and lesbian individuals held positions in government, but other
LGBTI individuals believed their orientation might be a barrier to entry into
government service.

HIV and AIDS Social Stigma

The National AIDS Commission is responsible for providing information,
programming, and campaigns on HIV/AIDS; however, no government body had
been tasked with providing specific services and advocacy.

Section 7. Worker Rights

a. Freedom of Association and the Right to Collective Bargaining

The law protects the right of workers to form and join unions of their choosing, the
right to strike, and bargain collectively, and the government generally respected
these. The labor code governs labor relations and employment regulations and
generally upholds international standards. The law prohibits dismissal or
discrimination for union activity, and it allows for financial compensation in lieu of
reinstatement. The law prohibits foreign migrant workers from participating in the
leadership of trade unions, but does not restrict their membership. The code does
not apply to workers in family-owned agricultural or industrial businesses used
primarily for subsistence, nor does it apply to civil servants.

There are official registration procedures for trade unions and employer
organizations. Workers employed by companies or institutions that provide
"indispensable social needs" such as pharmacies, hospitals, or telecommunications
firms are not barred from striking, but they are "obliged to ensure the provision of
minimal services deemed indispensable" to satisfy public needs during a strike.
The law allows the Council of Ministers to suspend a strike if it affects public
order. The law prohibits employer lockouts. There were two strikes during the
year, one against a Spanish company and one against a local company, over
employment contracts and salary entitlements. A union official noted that few
strikes occurred because workers faced extreme job insecurity, which encouraged
workers to seek mediation rather than risk losing work hours or their jobs.

The Secretary of State for Employment Policy and Vocational Training
(SEPFOPE) is the government agency charged with implementing the labor code
and labor dispute settlement. The government lacked sufficient resources and

skilled staff to enforce the right to freedom of association adequately. SEPFOPE and the trade union confederation registered more than 100 cases of alleged violations of labor rights between January and September, primarily against international companies. Most disputes arising under the labor code are settled through the mediation and conciliation service and the labor arbitration council. According to the strike law, workers must present claims in writing to their employer and give the employer five days to respond prior to declaring a strike. If the employers do not respond within that timeframe or respond but the parties do not reach agreement within 20 days, the organization representing the workers must provide the Civil Service Commission and SEPFOPE's General Labor Inspectorate five days' advance notice of a strike. Violations of the labor code are punishable by fines and other penalties, but they are not sufficient to deter violations. The confederation alleged that SEPFOPE's mediation procedures favored the employer. Alleged violations included salary discrimination, failure to provide maternity benefits, non-payment of wages, and unfair dismissal.

Workers' organizations were generally independent and operated without interference from government or employers. Unions may draft their own constitutions and rules and elect their representatives. A large portion of workers is not unionized in large part because the majority of workers are employed in the informal sector. Attempts to organize workers often were slowed by the fact that workers generally had little experience negotiating contracts, engaging in collective bargaining and negotiations, or otherwise securing their rights. During the year the confederation's campaign to promote collective bargaining enjoyed more success and less interference than in past years; it concluded agreements with more than 10 companies.

b. Prohibition of Forced or Compulsory Labor

The penal code criminalizes enslavement and prescribes penalties of between eight and 20 years' imprisonment. The penal code also considers forced labor and deceptive hiring practices ("trickery") to be a form of human trafficking, for which one may also receive eight to 20 years' imprisonment. SEPFOPE acknowledged it had insufficient human and financial capacity to enforce forced-labor laws.

The government established an Interagency Working Group to Combat Human Trafficking in April to coordinate implementation of a new national action plan.

Forced labor of adults and children occurred (see section 7.c.), but was not widespread.

Also see the Department of State's *Trafficking in Persons Report* at
www.state.gov/j/tip/rls/tiprpt/.

c. Prohibition of Child Labor and Minimum Age for Employment

The law prohibits child labor and specifically prohibits children under age 15 from
working, except at "light work" and in vocational training programs for children
between 13 and 15 years old. The labor law specifically outlaws all of the worst
forms of child labor and prohibits minors (defined as a person younger than age
17) from all forms of hazardous work, a definition that leaves 17-year-olds
vulnerable to child labor and exploitation. Child labor laws generally were not
enforced outside the capital. The labor code does not apply to family-owned
businesses operated for subsistence, the sector in which most children worked.
The government has not adopted a list of prohibited hazardous work.

The Ministry of Social Solidarity, SEPFOPE, and the PNTL are responsible for
enforcing child labor law. A lack of child labor professionals at SEPFOPE
hindered proper enforcement. Four of the government's 22 labor inspectors are
responsible for investigating child labor cases and enforcing child labor law, which
was inadequate to enforce restrictions on child labor. The Ministry of Social
Solidarity employed 29 child protection officers who could also refer cases to labor
inspectors. Inspectors are responsible for reporting cases of child labor and
working with relevant ministries, such as the Ministries of Health, Social
Solidarity, or Education, to provide services when children were identified.
Violations of child labor laws were referred for prosecution under the criminal
code.

There were no reports of any child labor or forced child labor-related prosecutions.
Penalties for child labor and forced labor violations may include fines and
imprisonment, but were insufficiently enforced to deter violations.

Child labor in the informal sector was a problem, particularly in agriculture, street
vending, and domestic service. The National Commission against Child Labor
conducts national assessments of child and forced labor, to identify and create a list
of work regarded as hazardous for children, and create a national action plan.

Although hard labor is uncommon for children, many children were expected to
work--either selling goods on the street, assisting in agriculture, or at menial tasks.
In rural areas, heavily indebted parents sometimes put their children to work as

indentured servants to settle debts. If the child is a girl, the receiving family could also demand any bride price payment normally owed to the girl's parents.

There were some reports of commercial sexual exploitation of children. Children in rural areas continued to engage in dangerous agricultural activities, such as cultivating and processing coffee in family-run businesses, using dangerous machinery and tools, carrying heavy loads, and applying harmful pesticides. Children were also employed in fishing, with some working long hours, performing physically demanding tasks, and facing other dangers such as drowning.

Also see the Department of Labor's *Findings on the Worst Forms of Child Labor* at www.dol.gov/ilab/reports/child-labor/findings/.

d. Discrimination with Respect to Employment and Occupation

The labor code prohibits discrimination based on color, race, civil status, gender, nationality, ethnic ancestry or origin, social position or economic status, political or ideological convictions, religion, physical or mental condition, age, or health status. The code also mandates equal pay. The government did not effectively enforce the code's provisions. Penalties are inconsistent and were not sufficient to deter violations, especially in the informal sector.

Employers may not require workers to undergo medical testing, including HIV testing, except with the worker's written consent. Work visa applications require medical clearance. There is no specific protection against discrimination based on sexual orientation.

Discrimination against women reportedly was common throughout the government, but sometimes went unaddressed. NGO workers noted that this was largely due to lack of other employment opportunities and fear of retaliation among victims. No reliable data was available on the problem. Women also were disadvantaged in pursuing job opportunities due to cultural norms, stereotypes, and an overall lower level of qualifications or education. The law offers no specific legal protection against discriminatory hiring practices due to marital status. Some reported that pregnant women did not receive maternity leave and other protections guaranteed by the labor code.

e. Acceptable Conditions of Work

The legally set minimum monthly wage is $115 (the U.S. dollar is the legal currency). The official national poverty level is $0.88 per day. Approximately half the population lived below the poverty line. The labor code provides for a standard workweek of 44 hours and standard benefits such as leave and premium pay for overtime. Overtime cannot exceed 16 hours per week, except in emergencies, which the labor code defined as "force-majeure or where such work is indispensable in order to prevent or repair serious damages for the company or for its feasibility." The law sets minimum standards for worker health and safety. The law provides explicitly for the right of pregnant women and new mothers to discontinue work that might harm their health without a cut in pay. It does not provide any other worker the right to leave a hazardous workplace without threat of dismissal. In addition paid maternity leave of 12 weeks is mandated, with compensated time for nursing up to six months. The law also requires five days of paid paternity leave. The law requires equal treatment and remuneration for all workers, including legally employed foreign workers.

The law covers all formal sectors except civil servants, defense and police force members, and family-owned businesses operated for subsistence. SEPFOPE is responsible for enforcement of the law. The law does not apply in the informal sector, which includes approximately 80 percent of the workforce. Domestic workers, a large percentage of the working population, especially of working women, were inadequately protected and particularly vulnerable to exploitative working conditions, with many receiving less than a living wage for long hours of work. The labor law states that domestic work is regulated by special legislation, which has not yet been adopted. The confederation advocated for the domestic worker law to provide additional protection to domestic workers. SEPFOPE acknowledged that it lacked staff and resources to provide effective protection. The annual budget for SEPFOPE's labor inspection section, which includes 22 inspectors, was insufficient to enforce the law adequately.

The labor code does not assign specific penalties or fines for violations of wage, hour, or occupational health and safety laws. A national labor board and a labor relations board exist, and there are no restrictions on the rights of workers to file complaints and seek redress. Labor unions criticized inspectors for visiting worksites infrequently and for only discussing labor concerns with managers during inspections.

According to a local union, the government lacked the political will and institutional capacity to implement and enforce the labor code fully, and violations of minimum safety and health standards were common.

According to SEPFOPE, labor laws, including those pertaining to hazardous work, do not apply to the informal sector.

The trade union syndicate indicated that there were at least three deaths at the port during the year due to unsafe workplace practices, and a Maritime Union of Australia assessment found that the port met none of the International Maritime Organization standards. Alleged violations of occupational health and safety standards were particularly common in the construction industry.